Abraham
Lincoln

Pocket **BIOGRAPHIES**

Series Editor C.S. Nicholls

Highly readable brief lives of those who have played a significant part in history, and whose contributions still influence contemporary culture.

Pocket BIOGRAPHIES

Abraham Lincoln

H.G. PITT

SUTTON PUBLISHING

First published in 1998 by
Sutton Publishing Limited · Phoenix Mill
Thrupp · Stroud · Gloucestershire · GL5 2BU

British Library Cataloguing in Publication Data
A catalogue record for this book is available from the British
Library

ISBN 0-7509-1511-0

 ALAN SUTTON™ and SUTTON™ are the
trade marks of Sutton Publishing Limited

Typeset in 13/18 pt Perpetua.
Typesetting and origination by
Sutton Publishing Limited
Printed in Great Britain by
The Guernsey Press Company Limited,
Guernsey, Channel Islands.

CONTENTS

For Stuart

CHRONOLOGY

1809	**9 February.** Born in Hardin County, Kentucky
1830	Leaves home to work in a store in New Salem
1832	**September.** Defeated in his first canvass
1834	Elected to the State Legislature
1836	Licensed as a lawyer
1837	Moves to Springfield, Illinois
1841	Stands down from the State Legislature
1842	Marries Mary Todd
1843	Birth of son Robert
1844	Establishes his own legal practice
1847	Takes up seat in Congress
1849	Returns to Illinois from Congress to concentrate on his legal practice
1850	Birth of son Willie
1853	Birth of son Thomas (Tad)
1854	Kansas-Nebraska Act allows slaves to be taken to new territory of Kansas. Re-awakens Lincoln's interest in politics
1856	Joins new Republican Party
1858	**August–October.** Series of public debates between Lincoln and Stephen A. Douglas in campaign to represent Illinois in the Senate
1860	Chosen as Republican Presidential candidate
1860	**20 December.** South Carolina secedes from the Union (the first of eleven states to do so)

1861	**4 March.** Inauguration as President
1861	**12 April.** Confederate attack on Fort Sumter. War starts between Confederate government and the Union in South Carolina
1861	**21 July.** Federal troops defeated at Bull Run
1862	**20 February.** Death of son Willie
1862	**18 April.** McClennan besieges the Confederate capital of Richmond, Virginia
1862	**22 September.** Victory for McClennan at Antietam
1862	**September.** Publication of the Emancipation Proclamation making slaves in rebellious states free
1863	**May.** Defeat at the hands of Confederate commander Robert E. Lee at Chancellorsville
1863	**July.** General Ulysses S. Grant takes Vicksburg for the Federal government
1863	**July.** Battle of Gettysburg
1863	**19 November** Gettysburg address
1863	**8 December.** Proclamation of Amnesty and Reconstruction for Louisiana and Tennessee
1864	**March.** Grant becomes General in Chief of the Union armies
1864	**June.** Lincoln renominated as Republican Presidential candidate
1864	**2 September.** Grant takes Atlanta
1864	Lincoln re-elected as President
1865	**31 January.** XIII Amendment passed by Congress abolishing slavery
1865	**9 April.** Lee surrenders to Grant
1865	**14 April.** Lincoln assassinated at the theatre

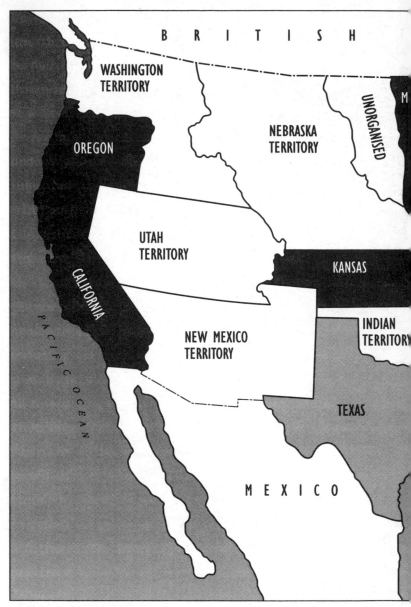

The United States, 1860/1

TERRITORIES

MINNESOTA

VERMONT

MAINE

LAKE SUPERIOR

NEW HAMPSHIRE

WISCONSIN

LAKE MICHIGAN

LAKE HURON

LAKE ONTARIO

MASS.

NEW YORK

RHODE ISLAND

IOWA

MICH

LAKE ERIE

PA.

Antietam

CONNECTICUT

New Salem

Gettysburg

NEW JERSEY

ILLINOIS

IND.

OHIO

DELAWARE

Springfield

Bull Run

Washington

MARYLAND

MISSOURI

OHIO River

KENTUCKY

VIRGINIA

Chancellorsville

MISSISSIPPI River

NORTH CAROLINA

TENNESSEE

Nashville

ARK.

SOUTH CAROLINA

MISS.

ALA.

GEORGIA

Charleston (Fort Sumter)

Vicksburg

Savannah

LOUISIANA

New Orleans

FLORIDA

ATLANTIC OCEAN

GULF OF MEXICO

miles

0   200   400

Free states   Slave states   Slave states loyal to the Union   Territories

THE EXPANSION
OF SLAVERY

On 4 March 1861 Abraham Lincoln took the oath as sixteenth President of the United States. Seven Southern states had seceded from the Union following his election in November; more were preparing to follow. The new President appealed to them:

> In *your* hands, my dissatisfied fellow countrymen, and not in *mine*, is the momentous issue of civil war. . . . *You* have no oath registered in Heaven to destroy the government, while *I* shall have the most solemn one to 'preserve, protect and defend' it. . . . We are not enemies, but friends. We must not be enemies. Though passion may have strained, it must not break our bonds of affection. The mystic chords of memory, streching [*sic*] from every battlefield, and patriot grave, to every living heart and hearthstone, all over this broad land, will yet swell the chorus of the

Union, when again touched, as surely they will be, by
the better angels of our nature.[1]

Six weeks later the war began. Only after 600,000
American lives had been lost would the broad land
be reunited. Four days after the guns fell silent, one
last bullet, fired by an assassin, ended the life of the
most peaceful of men who had fulfilled his oath to
'preserve and protect' his country.

In the half century since Abraham Lincoln had
been born in the western slave state of Kentucky in
1809 the United States had doubled in size. The
thirteen original states had grown to thirty-three
and the self-dependent local world had given way to
a huge market with railroads, canals, river-boats and
the telegraph supporting a continuously expanding
population and tying all the strands together. As the
frontier moved westward so the interests of the
various sectors of the country developed in
different ways and brought conflict which required
political solutions. Power was shared between the
Federal government and the governments of
the individual states – their relations were defined
by the Constitution of 1787. Ambiguities of
interpretation arose increasingly, ultimately to a

point where conflicting views could be resolved only by bloodshed.

In the North, hundreds of thousands of settlers had established small farms. By the middle of the century their surpluses of corn and hogs, which used to go down the Mississippi to New Orleans for shipment, were flowing back eastward on the railroads to feed the growing cities of the Atlantic seaboard. A natural east–west link was established in which hard work, self-help and individual enterprise were the key strengths. By contrast, the Southern states, bounded by the left banks of the two great rivers, Ohio and Mississippi, had grown into a patriarchal society dominated by large plantation owners who raised the valuable staple crops for markets abroad as well as at home: tobacco, rice, sugar and, above all, cotton which fed the insatiable hunger of the Lancashire mills.

The two sections – the North and the West, and the South – both complemented and conflicted with each other. The South earned foreign currencies with which America could buy its manufactured goods from Europe; the West still provided much of the South's agricultural needs. The North provided the capital needs of the planters, almost always

debtors. The South wanted free trade and easy
credit (and so opposed a regulating national bank).
Northern capitalists wanted tight control over
money supplies and a protective tariff to foster their
nascent industries. The West's interests swung to
and fro between them. These were the stuff of
politics – political parties which needed votes from
all sectors and interests worked to make compromises and find their way to power.

None of these conflicts of interest ever
threatened the Union. But there was one ingredient
of Southern society which marked it off sharply
from the rest of the country: slavery. The labour-
intensive plantations required large numbers of
low-status workers performing monotonous jobs all
the year round, whereas free farmers in the North
and West concentrated their work at certain seasons
– ploughing, planting and harvesting – the labour
for which was supplied by cooperation among the
farmers. The Americans did not invent slavery: it
had been universal in the thirteen colonies. But
during the eighteenth century religious and
enlightened views in Britain and the colonies
gradually came to regard slavery as morally
unacceptable.

The American Declaration of Independence of 1776 stated the same belief in equality and liberty: 'We hold these truths to be self-evident that all men are created equal, that they are endowed by their Creator with certain unalienable Rights, that among these are life, liberty, and the pursuit of Happiness.' However, when the Founding Fathers came to draw up the Federal Constitution in Philadelphia in 1787, the incompatibility of slavery with the Declaration of Independence was dodged. Their overriding concern was to make a 'more perfect union'. Divisive issues must be slurred over. Slavery was never mentioned by name but was protected in three provisions. First, the Constitution proclaimed that 'any one held to Service or Labour' who escaped must, if caught, be returned from a free state to his owner. Secondly, 'the Importation of such Persons as any of the States . . . shall think proper' should not be ended before 1808 (the slave trade was abolished the following year). And, thirdly, 'other persons' (those who are not free citizens) should count as three-fifths of a free person in the popular apportionment of representatives in the Congress. In 1791 the Xth amendment determined, 'The powers not delegated to the

United States by the Constitution nor prohibited by it to the States, are reserved to the States respectively, or to the people.'

So each state determined for itself whether it would tolerate slavery or not. Opponents of slavery hated these provisions but they recognized that, short of a revolution, there was nothing which could be done about them except by a constitutional amendment. And there were not enough people who minded about the slave to make that a possibility, whatever the Declaration of Independence said.

What was to bring about a civil war was not slavery, but the *expansion* of slavery. A free farmer could take his mule into any United States territories (from which the new states were being carved): could a slave-holder do the same with his slave? The Constitution was unclear: 'The Congress shall have Power to dispose of and to make all needful Rules and Regulations respecting the Territory, or other Property, of the United States.' Did that give Congress the power to *exclude* slavery – could exclusion be seen as a '*needful* rule'? If so then most of the vast unsettled areas might for ever be closed to the slave-owners. For the moment the question did not arise. Before 1820 new states tended to be admitted in pairs, one slave, one free. Neither slave-owner nor free farmer showed any wish to move into territory unless he thought it suitable for his kind of economy, plantation or small free farm. By that date slavery had been abolished in all the Northern and Western states, since it was not suitable for their economies, and the Federal government forbade it in territories north of the Ohio.

Then in 1820 the settlers in Missouri across the Mississippi, in territory extending further north than any existing slave state and lying right in the path of free settlers moving west from Illinois or south from Iowa, applied for admission as a slave state. At once moral anti-slavery sentiment was joined by a much larger body of opinion and interest which thought access to the territories should be open to all on equal terms. Free farmers, with little capital and no labour, could not hope to buy lots for themselves and their families in competition with the economic power of the slave-owners. In the ensuing crisis moral and economic hostility to slavery merged: it soon became impossible to distinguish motives. What has to be remembered is that those so-called 'free soilers' who opposed the *spread* of slavery were not necessarily opposed to slavery itself nor did they have much sympathy or liking for blacks, slave or free. They simply wished to exclude slavery (and blacks) from their backyards, now and in the future.

In the end Missouri was admitted as a slave state but as part of a Compromise in 1820 by which Congress excluded slavery from all other territory north of the latitude 36° 30'. (Congress could not exclude slavery from any new states made from such territory but it was highly unlikely that a territory peopled only by free settlers would then apply for admission as a slave state.) The next time slavery threw the nation into crisis Lincoln would be an active politician.

Abraham Lincoln grew up astride the Ohio, the divide between slave Kentucky, where he was born, and free Indiana and Illinois, where he lived until he went to the White House. His grandfather, a prosperous farmer, was killed by a roving Indian in 1786, leaving his younger son, Thomas, the victim of primogeniture, to fend for himself. By sheer hard work, Thomas acquired enough land in the sparsely settled frontier area to be able in 1807 to marry Nancy Hanks, the (perhaps illegitimate) daughter of Lucy Hanks. After a daughter, she gave birth to a son, Abraham, in their single room log cabin on 9 February 1809 in Hardin County. East Kentucky was poor land, with loose sandy soil under tough coarse grass. Life was unremitting toil, clearing and ploughing, planting and fencing, hunting bear and deer for meat and skins to make into clothing and shoes for the children. Social life, meagre though it was, turned on simple cooperation with neighbours at harvest time, sharing oxen and carts and log-rolling for building.

Abraham's parents had a simple Baptist faith which was opposed to slavery and to alcohol. They evaded the curse of drunkenness and the enthusiasm of frontier religion through the absence from the area of itinerant gospellers. Abraham never joined a church (as a young man he had taken off preachers for the entertainment of his friends); in 1864 he claimed that he had grown up 'naturally' with anti-slavery feelings. His earliest memories were of following his father as he planted corn, dropping pumpkin seeds in every other row. He attended a school for part of one year but at seven he could not read or write (his parents were illiterate). When he was seven the family moved across the Ohio to Pigeon Creek in South Indiana, 'as unpoetical as any spot of the earth' as Lincoln recalled it thirty years later.[2] The work of making a home and a farm was repeated. By the time he was eight the young Lincoln was wielding an axe, splitting logs for fencing, carrying water a mile, hunting small game and helping with the plough at harvest.

In the first year in Indiana, his mother and a great-aunt and uncle died. Perhaps he was remembering his grief then when he wrote to a young girl whose father had been killed in battle: 'sorrow comes to all; and, to the young, it comes with bitterest agony, because it takes them unawares. . . . I have had experience enough to know what I say.'[3] His father married again a year later, to Sarah Bush Johnston, a widow with three children. She was a strong, warm-hearted woman who provided a home for all five children and was dearly loved by the young Lincoln. She recollected after his death that they never had a cross word. Before he left for Washington, in 1860, he visited her: she had not wanted him to run for the Presidency because she feared for his safety. Lincoln consoled her, 'No no Mama, trust in the Lord and all will be well. We will See each other again.'[4] It was not to be.

After another short period at school – Lincoln remembered less than a year's schooling altogether – at last he could read and write. He devoured all he could find in print: the Bible, *Pilgrim's Progress*, Aesop's *Fables* and such Shakespeare as he could lay his hands on. His plain style of writing and speaking in later years was discovered for himself in these voyages into the world of the mind, of which he had had no previous experience. Always drawn to the great river, with its traffic making for the Mississippi, in 1828 he took the chance of sailing a cargo with a local store-keeper's son on a flat-boat to New Orleans, a thousand miles off. He left no account of his impressions of the bustling port of 40,000 inhabitants. Home after three months, he handed his meagre earnings to his father.

In 1830 his family moved again, this time to the good prairie land of Macon County in Illinois. Now of age, Lincoln was part of the caravanserai which

trudged the 200 miles north. On his return from
another trip to New Orleans, he left home for good
to work in a store in nearby New Salem, with no
clear purpose in mind, except that he did not wish
to follow his father on to the land.

LINCOLN'S ENTRY INTO POLITICS

Business in the store was light and left him time to read and enjoy the human library which gathered there. He was already famous in the little town of New Salem as a story-teller (sometimes a coarse one) and for the athletic skills of his powerful long-limbed physique; he soon stood at 6 ft 4 in, his size emphasized by the failure of his clothes to reach his ankles or his wrists. He was admired and wondered at for his self-reliance. Though entirely sociable, he kept his thoughts to himself. Men turned naturally to him for advice. After a year at the local debating society, he moved easily and light-heartedly into politics, where he could stretch his wits. His first canvass in 1832 was interrupted by his volunteering for the state militia in the Black Hawk war against local Indians trying to recover land they had ceded to the Federal government in

1804. Though he saw no action he claimed in 1860 that 'a success which gave me more pleasure than any I have had since' came when he was elected to command his troop of volunteers. Demobilized, he was defeated in September, 'the only time I have been beaten by the people'.[1] The following year he took work in a different store, which failed, was appointed the first local postmaster, where he was at the centre of local activity, and became Deputy Surveyor, travelling in the area laying out lots. In 1834 he was elected to the legislature for the first of four consecutive two-year terms.

Just at this time the conduct of public business was ceasing to be the haphazard affair in which voters' choices were affected more by personality than by platform or policy. Most states now had manhood suffrage. Organization was needed to see that some continuity was maintained. In 1828 the first populist candidate, Andrew Jackson, hero of the 1812 war against Britain, had been elected to the White House as the result of the first nationally managed campaign. His supporters called themselves Democrats. Those who feared that so adulated a figure might usurp the proper law-making role of Congress took the name of Whig, in memory of Parliament's resistance to King James II. If Jackson was to be beaten, they had no alternative but to imitate his machinery. By 1840 each party had a national convention, composed of elected delegates from all the state parties, who chose the presidential candidate and built a platform under him. So democracy and machine politics (i.e. politics managed by local political bosses) emerged simultaneously just as Lincoln appeared in the political world.

As in all democracies, all parties lived by ceaseless compromise and manoeuvring to attract the largest number of votes. But they were divided very loosely by different general attitudes. Democrats were for rapid expansion, easy credit, no Federal help for the states, which must manage their own internal improvements, and free trade; America's 'Manifest Destiny' was to carry democracy across to the Pacific (and perhaps elsewhere); and all immigrants should be welcome. The race must be to the swift with no advantages for the rich or the poor. By contrast, the Whigs were more cautious – they looked back to the probity and regulation of the earliest Federal administrators, when the voters followed the wisdom of their natural leaders, the wise and the true (and, oddly, the rich). They wanted a united economy, self-reliant, with new industries protected by tariffs, freeing America from the fluctuations of the European economies, whence came most of the country's manufactured goods. The Federal government should help the individual states and a national bank should regulate the currency to save the borrower from the constant collapse of under-capitalized state ventures. Territorial expansion should be controlled so that it did not outrun the interests or capacities of the existing Union. Voters inclined towards one party or the other according to how they saw their interests being affected at any particular moment.

Both parties had national followings, but there was one ingredient in the ethos of the Democrats which gave it a particular following which did not fluctuate according to circumstances. The Democrats believed in 'States' Rights' and a strict construction of the Constitution which limited the legitimate activities of the Federal government to a bare minimum. Above all, Democrats believed that the Federal government had no power over slavery – in the states or in the territories. As the strains over the expansion of slavery grew, so the Democrat Party became increasingly a party dominated by Southern 'slaveocrats'.

Lincoln entered politics as a Whig and the caution and moderation this implied stayed with him to the end. Why he joined the Whigs, who were very much a minority party in Illinois, is not clear. Hostility to slavery may have been an ingredient and perhaps at the beginning the chance to cut his teeth on the leading politicos of the state – not least Stephen A. Douglas, four years his junior, who rapidly established himself as a dominant Democrat. A foot shorter than Lincoln, the 'Little Giant' or 'Steam-engine in breeches' was to become Lincoln's greatest opponent.

Lincoln's experience of the local and intimate character of state politics and its immediacy to the voters was never forgotten. As President he would always keep his ear very close to the grass roots where the concerns of the voters reached him below the din of the politicians. Though he developed great manipulative skills he was never a 'machine' politician. He avoided taking sides among the party factions and all his real successes came from direct appeals to voters with whom he carefully guarded his reputation as honest and straightforward with plain and moving words. As President he rarely spoke publicly and he was an unimpressive impromptu orator; he preferred to express his views in the seeming intimacy of a private letter, which he would then ensure was published and circulated to party machines in the states.

The first indication of his feeling about slavery came in a protest he and another legislator entered in 1837 against a motion which had passed comfortably. Where the majority referred to the slave states' 'sacred' right to their property under the Constitution, the protesters substituted 'Congress . . . has no power under the Constitution to interfere with the institution of slavery in the different states' and 'the institution of slavery is founded on both injustice and bad policy'.[2] His moral condemnation of an institution while nevertheless acknowledging its protected status under the Constitution epitomized Lincoln's life-long view. He hated slavery; his respect for the Constitution was absolute.

In 1834, encouraged by a fellow legislator, Lincoln bought a copy of Blackstone's *Commentaries on the Laws of England* (at the same time he bought his first suit for sitting in the Legislature). Two years later, entirely self-taught, he was licensed as a lawyer and in 1837 moved to Springfield, the new state capital, which was to be Lincoln's home until he became President. Serving in two partnerships, he quickly built up a good practice based on his reputation for thoroughness and probity. In 1844 he set up on his own and took as his partner the twenty-six-year-old William Herndon, whom he liked for his liveliness and unquenchable intellectual curiosity. They were a complementary pair in a partnership that lasted until his death. Lincoln took on most of the itinerant business – twice a year, for ten weeks at a time, often astride 'Old Tom', he rode the 8th circuit with the itinerant judges who dispensed justice over 12,000 square miles, as often over tracks as on roads, where 6 miles an hour was good going. The lawyers stayed in primitive taverns, several to a room and very often sharing a bed. All the while Lincoln's circle of acquaintances widened and he was renowned for his good fellowship and the tall stories with which he entertained the local company. He became famous for his cross-examinations and in the late 1850s was regarded as the leading advocate in criminal cases in central Illlinois. In a murder case in 1858 he led a prosecution witness to give a graphic and detailed description of a murder observed by the light of a full moon. Lincoln pressed him for more detail. He then produced an almanac which showed that on the day and time alleged, the moon had already set.

He handled business of all sorts, frequently before the state Supreme Court: in 1841 he secured the freedom of a young free black woman who was wrongly being sold into slavery. Some years later he appeared unsuccessfully for a slave-owner who claimed the return of a runaway slave. In his legal practice Lincoln was guided by the law rather than by his moral sentiments. If the law were not paramount then there would be no security for either slave-owner or free man. This same fear of anarchy was apparent years later, at the root of his desire to restore civil government in the rebel states with the least delay: he well understood the dangers inherent in a situation in which 4 million newly free citizens suddenly appeared who had no conception of the law outside slavery.

In 1842 Lincoln married. The path to the altar had been a winding one. He was self-conscious and reticent with unmarried women, though he liked their company; he was more naturally at ease in male company which the conditions of frontier life encouraged. There are lacunae in our knowledge. A brief association with a girl in New Salem, who died suddenly in 1835, was said to have been the love of his life, leaving him desolate. A year later a broken engagement brought him low with an attack of 'hypo', his name for melancholia, which dogged him periodically all his life and which he considered a 'misfortune not a fault'.[3] In 1842 he married Mary Todd, daughter of Robert S. Todd, a well-to-do businessman in Lexington, Kentucky, and niece of the wife of a leading figure in Springfield. Privately educated, used to slaves as servants, with the graces of her background and a good conversationalist, her attractions for Lincoln resided in her established position and her charm. The difference in their rank and appearance was an attraction on both sides: her blue eyes, fair neck and arms, beneath a rather plain face contrasted with his ill-dressed, ungainly, tall frame with its gnarled features and mop of rough hair. Life for Mary now changed considerably. They lived in hotels until 1844 when her husband bought a small house, where he tended his own horse, milked the cow and cut and carried the firewood. She bore him four sons between 1843 and 1853. The eldest, Robert, was never very close to his father whom he outlived by fifty years; Edward died in 1850; and the dearly loved 'Willie' (born in late 1850) died in the White House at the age of eleven, a devastating loss to both his parents. Mary never got over her grief but Lincoln became very close to Thomas, known as Tad, born in 1853, who was to be his constant companion in the White House, a boy loved all the more for his cleft palate and crooked teeth. He outlived his father, but only by six years.

The marriage was uneasily happy but never intimate, sometimes disrupted by Mary's violent temper (when Lincoln thought it wise to leave the house till it had subsided). She caused Lincoln embarrassment by her tendency to live beyond their means – Lincoln felt bound to repay part of the cost of furnishings she bought for the White House at the expense of the Federal Government. He was too busy earning to keep his family to have much time for social activity. Left to himself, he was by nature quiet and reflective and too occupied or unobservant to appreciate the domestic burden Mary bore. She was extrovert, sociable and liked to attract attention. As President's wife she enjoyed the social responsibilities of her position but was criticized for her extravagance in wartime and was affected by the sad divisions of her family — she had one brother in each of the opposing armies and three half-brothers in the Confederate army, two of whom were killed. Though their relations were formal — he was 'Mr Lincoln' and, after Robert's birth, she was always 'Mother' — they were devoted and loyal to each other and she was very proud of him and would admit no criticism.

THREE

LINCOLN IN CONGRESS

In 1841 Lincoln stood down from the state legislature to concentrate on his legal practice. By 1843 he was admitting 'The truth is I would like to go [to Congress] very much'.[1] Three years later he got the nomination of his county and was elected to the House, taking his seat in December 1847. (The new Congress meets in the December of the year following its election.)

Lincoln arrived in the middle of a new row about expansion and, soon, about slavery. The 'lone star' republic of Texas, which had established its independence from Mexico, had for nine years been seeking admission to the United States. Finally in 1845 Congress annexed it to the US and admitted it as a state. Northern Whigs were uneasy about the admission: Texas was twice the size of any other state and already a slave state. Lincoln objected, less because of the slavery than because the annexation of new territories at the whim of impulsive local settlers was very like 'mobocracy'. Within a year a smouldering frontier dispute with Mexico resulted in a war from which America emerged with huge conquests, comprising the present California, New Mexico, Utah, Colorado, Nevada and Arizona. Lincoln opposed the war (but voted supplies once it had started), thinking it better to cultivate and civilize what America already possessed, 'making it a garden, improving the morals and education of the people'.[2]

Annexation of these vast areas revived the crisis over slavery after thirty years. In those years the population of the United States had grown rapidly: free states like Illinois, Indiana and Ohio had previously been peopled largely by settlers, like the Lincolns, coming north across the Ohio from the slave states. Now new floods of immigrants were crossing the Appalachians and coming down the Ohio or south from the Great Lakes: 87 per cent of the 3 million who came to America in the decades after 1846 settled in the free states. They were largely indifferent to slavery among their Southern neighbours – that was their business, adapted to their economic needs and a system of race control. But what these westward-flowing families did not want was to find their newest territories being denied to them by the presence of slavery and slave-owners who could afford to buy up the best lots and leave them to sink into the class of 'dirt' farmers, 'po' whites', which was the lot of so many non-slave-owners in the South. Objections to slavery in the mid-Western states did have a moral ingredient, but the driving energy was territorial and did not imply sympathy for blacks, slave or free (Illinois amended its constitution in 1853 to prohibit the residence in the state of free negroes).

From 1846 free soilers, those opposed to the spread of slavery, pushed unavailingly in Congress to prohibit slavery in any newly acquired territory. In 1848, swelled by the rush for gold, California applied for admission as a free state. The South objected to any limitation of the spread of slavery and to the admission of California. After two years of bitter wrangling the Union was saved by a Compromise: California was to be admitted free; a new Fugitive Slave Act (Northern states were refusing to implement the old one) was put under Federal operation and juries dispensed with; and as the newly acquired territories, subdivided no doubt, came to apply for admission as states, they should come in with or without slavery as their constitution prescribed at the moment of application. The Compromise did not make clear whether an elected *territorial* government could exclude slavery (so predetermining the decision the new *state* would take). The Compromise of 1850 was a desperate effort to take the heat out of the slavery question by turning it into a mere local matter, to be decided by those most immediately affected on the ground. Paradoxically, if it had been possible to get Americans to agree that slavery was only a concern for the locals such a compromise would not have been necessary. The fear that the only way any agreement could be reached was by the localizing device of 'popular sovereignty', as local choice was called, was a sure guarantee that the settlers' choice, whenever it came, would agitate the whole nation. Slavery was *not* a local issue; it was *the* national concern, morally and economically, whenever its expansion was at issue. The Constitution could not help: there was no agreement as to whether controlling slavery in the territories was a 'needful rule and regulation' or not. Few politicians had confidence that slavery could remain a matter of mere parish pump interest for long. Anti-slavery agitation in the North was now creating a conviction in the Southern mind that all Americans north of the Ohio were abolitionists for whom limiting the spread of slavery was only a device to rid America of the institution altogether. The publication of Harriet Beecher Stowe's sentimental *Uncle Tom's Cabin* in 1852, the only work of near-literature in the whole long crisis, and the laws passed in several Northern legislatures forbidding their citizens to cooperate with Federal authorities in apprehending fugitive slaves, so defying the new fugitive slave law, confirmed Southern suspicions and seemed to prove their point.

In all this Lincoln, who had returned to Illinois from Congress in 1849 to nurture his law practice, showed little interest. In a eulogy in 1852 of Henry Clay, the great Whig leader who had played an important part in settling the 1850 crisis, he castigated the opponents of the settlement for destabilizing the Union. He retained his moral objection to slavery but insisted on the supremacy of the Constitution which protected existing slavery. He quoted Jefferson's fearful words of years before: 'We have the wolf by the ears and we can neither hold him, nor safely let him go. Justice is in one scale, and self-preservation in the other.'[3]

Lincoln hoped that the slavery question had now been set aside. The unceasing pressure for western expansion made sure that it was not. For a long time settlers had been pressing forward to cross the Mississippi, from Missouri (a slave state since 1820) and from free Iowa, into the huge unorganized territory known only as Nebraska. Simultaneously there was quickening pressure for a trans-continental railroad to California. (A railroad could not run through unorganized territory — Indians were too prone to remove the telegraph wires to use in their bows.) Where the eastern terminus of such a line might be would determine the economic future of a whole area. The Senate chairman of the Committee on Territories, whose task it would be to see any provision for the area through Congress, was Stephen A. Douglas, Senator for Illinois and the most powerful Northern Democrat in Congress, already well known to Lincoln. He had been the broker of the clutch of bills in the 1850 settlement and had every prospect of the Democratic nomination in 1856, having missed it in 1852. A pragmatist who saw nothing in the slavery question which need bother the American conscience, he believed that in 'popular sovereignty' lay the universal solvent. He presented a bill for the organization of Kansas (the area adjacent to Missouri) and Nebraska (to the north of Kansas) to Congress in December 1853. As a Chicagoan he hoped that the opening up of these lands would forward the interests of Illinois in the contest to be the starting point for the western railroad. The bill was immediately criticized because it said nothing about who could go into the territory with their property. The whole area of Kansas and Nebraska fell under the provisions of the Missouri Compromise which banned slavery in territory north of 36° 30'. The 1853 bill said the territory should be admitted eventually as a state with or without slavery as its proposed state constitution provided, but that would be little comfort to slave-holders if they had been banned from entry to help shape that constitution. Eventually the dominant Democratic Southern Congressmen and Senators forced Douglas to amend the bill, explicitly repealing the

Missouri Compromise. As a price for continued Southern support for the transcontinental projects and organization of the new territory, Douglas ingeniously argued that the limitations imposed by the Missouri Compromise in 1820 had already been 'superseded' by the new principles of 'popular sovereignty' provided for the ex-Mexican territories in the 1850 Compromise. The fact that the 1850 provision had applied only to territories acquired long after the Compromise of 1820 and that no one, in 1850, had noticed that 'popular sovereignty' was to be considered a new principle applicable to all territory of the United States was pushed aside and Douglas's later proposals, known as the Kansas-Nebraska Act, were forced through with predominantly Southern support. Slaves could now be taken into Kansas.

The uproar which followed was immediate and proved to be the point of no return for rising sectional hostilities. Though there was nothing unconstitutional in repealing the Missouri Compromise, the repeal was regarded by the free states as a violation of a sacred compact hallowed by time which had settled for ever how far north slavery could come. The pro-slavery interests argued that the 1820 Compromise had always been illegal because it violated the principle that the territories were the common property of all American states and that all citizens should have equal rights therein: if a free farmer could take his mule into a territory, why could a slave-owner not take his slaves in? Both were forms of property recognized and protected by the law.

In 1820 and 1850 the crises had been resolved by compromises – like all good compromises they were more practical than pleasing to both parties. But they had held. The novelty of the Kansas Nebraska bill was that it revoked a previous settlement and represented a victory for one side. The effect was a political revolution which replaced the old universal parties, whose votes straddled the Ohio river, with two parties, one of which was specifically sectional and the other increasingly so. The old Whig party, already moribund, collapsed, and its Southern wing was slowly absorbed into the Democratic party which now represented the slavery interest. Northern Whigs and large numbers of Northern Democrats coalesced into a new Republican party committed specifically to ending the further spread of slavery.

Paradoxically what Douglas had most feared –
the emergence of sectional politics – had now taken
firm hold. Douglas was right: slavery could be
defused by popular sovereignty, but only if everyone
ceased to have strong feelings about it. In the event,
Douglas's actions intensified rather than quieted the
national concern about slavery.

Lincoln, now out of active politics, moved
cautiously: as he put it in an autobiographical
sketch for the 1860 campaign, 'I was losing interest
in politics, when the repeal of the Missouri
Compromise aroused me again'.[4] In that crisis he
discovered a cause and a moral energy which
turned him from a local politician with few
ambitions and a successful law practice into a
statesman who held his cause to its principles
through the vicissitudes of civil war. By the autumn
he had moved from a tolerance of American
slavery as a sad inhumane fact to a full moral
condemnation of it: 'Is not slavery universally
granted to be, in the abstract, a gross outrage of the
law of nature? . . . Is it not held to be the great
wrong of the world?'[5] He insisted on a distinction
between slavery where it already existed and was
constitutionally protected and its extension into

new areas, to which he was totally hostile. He laid no blame: 'I have no prejudice against the Southern people. They are just what we would be in their situation. If slavery did not exist among them, they would not introduce it. If it did now exist among us we should not instantly give it up.' He saw the intractability of the problem: 'If all earthly power were given me, I should not know what to do, as to the existing institution.'[6] But he could see no excuse for spreading slavery further: 'No man is good enough to govern another man, *without that other's consent*. I say this is the leading principle – the sheet anchor of American republicanism.'[7]

Now Lincoln's interest turned again to politics. Privately he wrote, 'I have really got it into my head to try to be a United States senator.' The following February internal party quarrels deprived him of the opportunity. By May 1856, by which time some two hundred people had died in the 'local' argument about slavery in Kansas, Lincoln joined the new Republican party, the coalition of former Whigs and Democrats who pledged themselves to resisting the spread of slavery. At its first national bid for the Presidency in 1856 the party lost to the Pennsylvania Democrat, James Buchanan.

Two days after the new President's inaugural speech the Supreme Court, as the arbiter of the Constitution, delivered a deeply divisive judgement. In a case concerning the plea of a slave, Dred Scott, for his freedom, Chief Justice Taney gave the majority opinion of the court. No negro could plead in a Federal court because no negro (slave or free) had ever been, or could be, a citizen (the case could have stopped here). Instead, the court went on to rule that, since no citizen could be deprived of his property except by due process of law, Congress could not ban slavery from the territories. The effect of this was to declare the Missouri Compromise unconstitutional after thirty-six years of accepted operation. Further, since Congress could not exclude slavery from the territories neither could any territorial legislature (since the legislature was the creation of Congress). This invalidated the 'popular sovereignty' principles enshrined in both the 1850 and 1854 Acts. The only institution which could legislate on slavery was the state when it emerged from its territorial shell.

Free soilers at once suspected a conspiracy to 'nationalize' slavery. If all property was equal and its rights absolute, how could a free state confiscate a slave-owner's property if he chose to come among them with it? Lincoln clung to his constitutionalism, accepted judicial review of Congressional law by the Supreme Court, but insisted that the judgement only applied to the particular case before the court: the decision was a bad one and he would attempt by constitutional means to get it reversed. Douglas, equally angered, argued that, while the court could uphold the rights of slave-holders, if the people of a territory did not want slavery they could exclude it simply by passing unfriendly legislation or denying slave-holders police protection: 'Slavery could not exist for a day or an hour' without protective legislation.

In 1858 Douglas was up for re-election as one of the senators for Illinois. Lincoln set out to defeat him in the most famous series of debates in America's history.

FOUR

A HOUSE DIVIDED
AGAINST ITSELF
CANNOT STAND

Illinois was a microcosm of the nation: it had historic links to the slave states across the Ohio and down the Mississippi and its rapidly expanding northern half, commercially linked to the east coast, was home to numerous liberal refugees, especially Germans, from the 1848 Revolutions. At his adoption in June 1858 Lincoln starkly declared his position, more provocatively than lucidly. With a startling, Biblical simile which, once heard, would never be forgotten, he insisted that the agitation over slavery

> *will* not cease, until a *crisis* shall have been reached, and passed. 'A house divided against itself cannot stand.' I believe this government cannot endure, permanently, half *slave* and half *free*. I do not expect

the Union to be *dissolved* – I do not expect the house to *fall* – but I *do* expect it will cease to be divided. It will become *all* one thing, or *all* the other.[1]

Southern 'fire-eaters' understood the writing on the wall: either slavery must expand or it would in time be hemmed in by new free states, numerous enough in the fullness of time to provide the three-quarters of the states necessary to pass an amendment to the Constitution outlawing slavery. There could be no protection for existing slavery except by its expansion.

Lincoln, who might draw small audiences and little attention on his own, persuaded Douglas to agree to joint debates at seven sites around the state between August and October: the speakers would alternate in opening for an hour, replying for an hour and a half and then the first speaker would have half an hour for his rejoinder. The requirement that all political argument must square with the Constitution put a premium on fine points and careful argument to which two such highly respected lawyers were accustomed. The debates drew huge crowds of tens of thousands which often arrived in special trains. Encouraged by hard cider and a carnival air, they followed the intricate arguments with cries of 'You've got him', 'Hit him again', 'Give it to him', while a crowd of reporters saw that verbatim accounts appeared in national newspapers. The campaign produced the greatest political debate since the Constitutional Convention in 1787. Its immediate effect was to turn Lincoln, though the loser, barely then a politician, into a national figure and the flag-bearer of Republican ideology.

Much of the detail of the debates ploughed repetitiously over recrimination and accusations of skullduggery in the state politics of the candidates. Douglas' difficulties with his own party over popular sovereignty were played on by Lincoln, though he had to be careful not to show just how much Douglas differed from the Democratic administration, lest it encourage those eastern Republicans who believed that the powerful Douglas would make a better opponent to the extension of slavery than the inexperienced novice Lincoln. But crucial distinctions between the two men soon emerged. Douglas insisted that the issue was democracy, the right of voters to decide for themselves how they wished to be governed. Only local popular sovereignty could ensure that. Slavery, in itself, was of no interest. It only impinged on the lives of those men who lived near it. Douglas cared not whether slavery was voted up or down: 'I care more for the great principle of self-government, the right of the people to rule, than I do for all the negroes in Christendom.'[2] 'This government was established on the white basis. It was made by white men, for the benefit of white men and their posterity for ever . . . [the negro belongs] to a race incapable of self government, and for that reason ought not to be on an equality with white men' (immense applause).[3] The moral meaning of the great American experiment lay in the pursuit of manifest destiny, 'that great mission, that destiny which Providence has marked out for us . . . filling up our prairies, clearing our wildernesses and building cities, . . . and thus [making] this the asylum of the oppressed of the whole earth.'[4] Was this great moral endeavour and its instrument, the Union, to be thrown away to satisfy the meddling fantasies of Black Republicans (as Douglas always called Lincoln's party) who perverted the intentions of the Founding Fathers and insisted that diversity of institutions must give way to an enforced conformity which would destroy the whole edifice?

Lincoln went back to first principles: the Declaration of Independence meant what it said and had a universal and perpetual application. To live by its assertions made America a contining aspiration as well as an achievement. Though slavery had been accepted of necessity in 1787 the Founding Fathers had always hoped and expected that it would die out, and in the North West Ordinance of 1787 they had forbidden its expansion into the then territories of the United States. 'The real issue in this controversy is the sentiment on the part of one class that looks upon the institution of slavery *as a wrong*, and of another class that *does not* look upon it as a wrong. . . . Is it not a false statesmanship that undertakes to build up a system of policy upon the basis of caring nothing about *the very thing that everybody does care the most about?*'[5] In envisaging the end of slavery Lincoln raised the equally difficult question of what freedom and equality would mean for the free negro. Taunted by Douglas that he was a negro lover and ultimately a miscegenist, Lincoln had to tread warily. He denied that he wanted the black to be a citizen, voting and holding office, to sit on juries, or to marry a white (Lincoln supported the laws in Illinois which forbade intermarriage).

> I agree with Judge Douglas [the negro] is not my
> equal in many respects – certainly not in color,
> perhaps not in moral or intellectual endowment. But
> in the right to eat the bread, without leave of
> anybody else, which his own hand earns, *he is my*
> *equal and the equal of Judge Douglas, and the equal of*
> *every living man.*[6]

Both men agreed that decisions about the blacks
should be taken by white men, but they could not
agree where, in a federal constitution, those
decisions should be made. For both men the Union
was of paramount significance – but for Lincoln that
Union would be no union if it built into its future a
denial of those very principles of liberty in which it
had originally been grounded.

In the election Douglas carried a majority of the
constituencies which then, in the new legislature,
sent him to the Senate; Lincoln carried the popular
vote by a small margin. Nationally, Lincoln had
raised the discussion of what was at stake to a high
moral level and shown himself to be a worthy
opponent of the country's most formidable orator.
(He described Douglas's continued support of
popular sovereignty, after its disallowance by Chief
Justice Taney's decisions as 'got down as thin as the

homoeopathic soup that was made by boiling the shadow of a pigeon that had starved to death'.)[7]

Though Lincoln returned to his law business after his defeat, this time his political activities did not abate: he continued speaking all over the Western states to keep the moral reasons for Congressional restriction on slavery expansion firmly in voters' minds lest they retreated into acceptance of Douglas's easy blandishments that popular sovereignty could remove all the tension in the slavery question. Without the moral imperative the Republican party had no reason for existence. If that was lost, the whole battle would have to be fought all over again. In September 1859, in a rare speech not concerned with slavery, Lincoln set out his views of how a free state should work. From a labour theory of value he saw individual freedom and self-respect as emerging from a competitive free market (and no free man should be so placed that he had to compete unfairly beside a slave). Economic independence was the goal and in the great expanding economy every man could achieve it: every man had the chance to pull himself up over the mud-sill in which the slave is forever condemned to work for others. Labour is prior to capital, capital is the fruit of labour: the speaker himself had been a hired man twenty-eight years previously, but was now working for himself. There is no such thing as a freeman being fatally fixed for life. Free labour required free soil — a free homestead granted in the national domain by the Federal government and soil free from the obstruction of slavery. Free Men, Free Labour and Free Soil was the epitome of Republican appeal. Lincoln's views exactly suited the condition and aspirations of the Western farmer but they had little resonance now for the labour force in the Eastern cities where economic independence was less likely any longer to be the reward for hard work.

In the summer of 1859 Lincoln's thoughts turned towards the Presidential election in the following year. In a private letter he wrote, 'I must say I do not think myself fit for the Presidency'.[8] In a short biography he authorized in late December he stressed his poor, rural, self-educated, self-made progress. He never made any claim to have influenced public affairs or to have taken sides on any issue before 1854. He was (most conveniently and happily) a man without a controversial past. Back home in April 1860, after a very successful first speaking tour in the East, he admitted to Senator Trumball (who had been elected in his stead in 1855), 'the taste *is* in my mouth a little'.[9] He took great care in seeing a complete edition of his debates with Douglas through the press: they became a best-seller on the eve of the Republican Convention at Chicago in May. Lincoln was pushed by the Illinois delegation as the self-made man, representative of free labour: 'Honest Abe' the rail-splitter [log-splitter]. He was presented as a moderate who rejected the 'Irrepressible Conflict' and 'Higher Law' of William H. Seward, the leading contender for the nomination: 'Our policy . . . is to give no offence to others – leave them in a mood to come to us, if they shall be compelled to give up their first loves.'[10] On the fourth ballot Lincoln got the necessary absolute majority when Ohio, abandoning its own eminent contender, Governor Samuel P. Chase, threw its decisive votes to Lincoln. A moderate platform was built under him: internal improvements (for the West), a restrained tariff plank (essential to win Pennsylvania and New Jersey), no restrictions on immigration (to satisfy the Germans) and support for a Pacific railroad. The right of each state to determine its own domestic institutions was reaffirmed. Moral condemnation of slavery was avoided.

After the convention he was publicly silent, but privately he urged caution: the party, an amalgam of all the older parties, needed all the votes it could get. 'The point of danger is the temptation in different localities to "*platform*" for something which will be popular just there, but . . . a firebrand elsewhere. . . . In a word, in every locality we should look beyond our noses; and at least say *nothing* on points where it is probable we shall disagree.'[11]

His most decisive action during the campaign was to grow a beard – the first president to do so – in response to a promise from an eleven-year-old girl that she would then persuade her brother to vote for him. 'As to the whiskers,' he replied, 'having never worn any, do you not think that people would call it a piece of silly affection (*sic*) if I were to begin now?'[12] He took the risk.

The only man who could (and almost certainly would) win the election for the Democrats was Lincoln's old rival Stephen Douglas. But he was hated now by the President, for his defiance of the administration's attempt to admit Kansas as a state

with slavery, and by a core of 'fire-eaters', for whom
there was no solution to the sectional problem short
of secession. The party in convention now split,
Douglas was nominated and the 'fire eaters'
produced their own candidate, making it clear that
their states would leave the Union if Lincoln was
elected. A Republican victory would be an
indication of the future. Since, as they understood
it, the whole economy and social structure of their
slave states depended on slavery, no sovereign state
(as they believed themselves to be) could stay in a
voluntary union which in the end must destroy it.
The time to assert independence was now, before it
was too late. A party called Constitutional Unionists
emerged in the Western states, with a single plank –
'the Constitution of the Country, the Union of
States and the enforcement of the laws'. Their
attraction was strong in the border states: if war
came their farms and towns would be the military
field; the ideologues, North or South, safe in their
beds in Boston or Charleston, had no such fears to
temper their principles.

In 1860, with the vote split four ways, Lincoln
was elected by 42 per cent of the popular vote, and
by 180 to the Southern fire-eaters' 72 votes in the

electoral college. Douglas, with 31 per cent of the popular vote, carried only two states. (This brave, tough fighter who, tradition has it, held Lincoln's hat when the new President took the oath, and who believed always that popular sovereignty alone could take the heat out of the sectional crisis, was dead by December of 1861 – until then he gave unstinted support to his old opponent.)

The Southern states now prepared to leave the Union. For four months Lincoln could only watch disaster unfold.

FIVE

SLAVERY AND SECESSION

Determined not to compromise his public position, Lincoln kept a public silence as the Union crashed out of control. The outgoing President, James Buchanan, in his last annual message to Congress, blamed the whole crisis on Republican agitation against slavery. He declared secession to be unconstitutional and then went on to argue that the Federal government lacked any constitutional authority to prevent it. This left Congress as the only hope for a peaceful settlement. There the most promising proposal was to extend the line of 36° 30' to the west coast in all existing territory 'now held or hereafter to be acquired' and guarantee the Southern area to slavery by a constitutional amendment. Many moderate Republicans, grasping at a straw, were inclined to agree. Lincoln was adamant: privately, he wrote, 'on the territorial question . . . I am inflexible . . . the tug has to come, and better now, than any time hereafter.'[1] Thus strengthened, the Republicans in Congress rejected the proposal: no state should be able to set conditions on which it stayed in the Union. On 20 December South Carolina seceded, the first of seven states to go before Lincoln took office: Florida, Georgia, Alabama, Mississippi, Louisiana and Texas followed.

Federal coastal forts in South Carolina and Florida were running short of provisions. The government could not now do nothing. To evacuate the forts would be to recognize the right of secession; to attempt to supply them might precipitate war. A ship sent by Buchanan in early January 1861 to Fort Sumter in Charleston harbour was fired on by shore batteries and turned away. The guns in the fort remained silent. The fuse had been lit and smouldered on until Lincoln took office on 4 March. In his inaugural address Lincoln repeated that his government posed no threat to slavery in the states and promised it would not attempt to re-occupy Federal property already seized, but he reiterated that the Union was perpetual and could not be

Lincoln: the first known photograph, 1846. (Photograph: Lloyd Ostendorf, Dayton, Ohio)

Lincoln's house in Springfield, with Tad and Willie, 1860. (Photograph: Lloyd Ostendorf, Dayton, Ohio)

'The little Giant.' Stephen A. Douglas, Lincoln's opponent in the 1858 debates. (Photograph: Lloyd Ostendorf, Dayton, Ohio)

Campaigning in New York, February 1860. (Photograph: Lloyd Ostendorf, Dayton, Ohio)

The first 'First Lady'. Mary Lincoln dressed for a ball, 1861. (Photograph: United States National Archives, III-B-5864)

The President visits the Army: facing McClellan after Antietam, October 1862. (Photograph: Library of Congress, LC-B8171-7951)

'Grant is mine and I am his till the end of the war.' Ulysses S. Grant, commander of all the Union armies, spring 1864. (Photograph: © Hulton Getty)

Unfinished business. The Capitol at Lincoln's second Inauguration, 4 March 1865.
(Photograph Lloyd Ostendorf, Dayton, Ohio)

'With malice toward none, with charity for all.' The last photograph, spring 1865.
(Photograph: Lloyd Ostendorf, Dayton, Ohio)

'All seems well with us', from Our Special War Correspondent. This Thomas Nast cartoon was published in *Harper's Weekly* the day of Lincoln's assassination. (Photograph: Lloyd Ostendorf, Dayton, Ohio)

dissolved except by consent: 'The central idea of secession is the essence of anarchy. A majority, held in restraint by constitutional checks, . . . is the only true sovereign of a free people. Whoever rejects it, does, of necessity, fly to anarchy or to despotism.'[2] The linking of national integrity to popular government – an alliance crucial to contemporaneous liberal movements in Italy and Germany – was central to Lincoln's philsophy and determined his policy until his death. Whatever strain the present crisis brought, democratic government had to rise to surmount it. To abandon popular government, even to preserve the Union, would be defeat because popular consent was the foundation on which the whole edifice of the Union rested.

Two days into office Lincoln learned that Fort Sumter had supplies for only six weeks. Under the Constitution the executive power resides singly in the President. His ministers are advisers only; he can consult them or not as he wishes. The extent of his powers in wartime, as Commander-in-Chief of the Army and Navy, he alone could determine by his oath to 'preserve, protect and defend the Constitution'. Lincoln had no interval to ease himself into the job. He put his cabinet together immediately, the higher offices going to the most experienced Republican politicians, three of whom had sought the nomination themselves. When he first consulted the cabinet only one member agreed that supplies should be sent to Fort Sumter; the General-in-Chief, Winfield Scott, hero of the Mexican War, now seventy-four and ill, had already told Lincoln that the fort could not be held. William H. Seward, his Secretary of State, in private negotiation with Southern commissioners, had left them with a strong impression that Sumter would be abandoned. Meanwhile Northern opinion clamoured for action. On 29 March (after a sleepless night), now with the agreement of all but two of his cabinet, Lincoln ordered two expeditions to be prepared to sail to Sumter and to Fort Pickens (in Florida). Seward, at once, in a private letter to Lincoln, proposed that Spain and France should be provoked into war to reunite the nation and divert the secession movement: 'It must be somebody's business to pursue and direct. . . . It is not in my especial province; But I neither seek to evade nor assume responsibility.'[3] This challenge to his own responsibility from the most senior of his ministers was met by Lincoln with a reasoned but sharp reply: 'if this must be done, *I* must do it . . . I wish, and suppose I am entitled to have the advice of all the cabinet.'[4] He then never sent it but kept a copy in his desk, a device he often used, to calm his anger and sort out his own ideas. He was never again challenged by Seward who became his closest and most admiring supporter.

On 4 April 1861 Lincoln ordered the expedition to Sumter to sail. The Confederate government (as the seven seceded states had now constituted themselves) was warned that Sumter was about to be provisioned peacefully and would fire only if attacked. As the ships neared Charleston harbour the shore guns opened up on the fort in the early hours of 12 April, and the Federal garrison replied. The provisioning fleet could offer no help. After thirty hours of bombardment the fort surrendered. No one had died on either side, but the war had started and, by luck or by Lincoln's astute provocation, the rebels had fired the first shot. The President now assumed his full responsibility to defend the Union against its enemies.

Neither side wanted war. Nor was war the only possible outcome: compromises had contained the quarrel previously, why not now? Or why should the rebel states not be given what they sought — independence? Nothing in the stars required that the United States must remain a single entity: encouraged by liberals, the emergence of new nations out of larger and older states had been the pattern of change in nineteenth-century Europe.

Many in the North, fearing the disruption of their interests in the event of war, wanted to 'let the erring sisters go', which would also have released the Northern conscience from the taint of responsibility for the continuation of slavery.

In all this Lincoln was the crucial figure. His belief in the Union and in democracy was absolute. To ignore the decision of the electorate — that slavery should be contained — would be a destruction of the Union. It is difficult to believe that if any of the other contenders for the Republican nomination had been chosen and gone on to win the election he would not have accepted, in some form or other, either the fact (as it now was) of secession or a reconstruction of the Union which would have constitutionally guaranteed a future for slavery and its expansion. Neither outcome would have been dishonourable. Slavery itself was not at issue: was it worth the lives of half a million Americans just to force the containment of slavery? At the start no one believed that the war was about slavery, the security of which Lincoln stressed again and again: it was simply a war to restore the Union as it was before South Carolina seceded. With hindsight, the rightness of Lincoln's decision, and it was his, remains disputable, but its consequences for posterity were momentous and benign. The Republican cause triumphed, not only on the battlefield, but in the minds of men: America emerged, with its commitment to the ideal that all men are created equal, battered but intact. The consequences for the whole of mankind if Lincoln had decided otherwise or had lost his courage in the darkest days of the war does not long bear contemplation.

Lincoln assembled a cabinet which combined all his rivals together with representatives of the key states. He then left ministers to run their departments without interference. Their conflicting views and interests he turned to his advantage: his own complete immunity from a compromising political past left him free to lean to one side or the other as circumstances required. He had no axe to grind except seeing that the war was won. In his four years he made almost no cabinet changes. Though politically an extremely skilled manipulator, his openness and lack of personal objectives enabled him to get things done without loss of countenance or respect. His use of his cabinet was haphazard: he arrived at all his major decisions on his own by slow rumination and preferred talking with individual members of the cabinet rather than with the whole body. He was reluctant and wily about expressing policy – he remained 'shut-mouth' until he had arrived at a decision and he asserted, more than once, that, 'I have no policy; my hope is to save the Union. I do the best I can today in the hope that when tomorrow comes I am ready for its duty.'[5] As he reflected in his last year, 'It was a time when a man with a policy would have been fatal to the country'. He was a patient listener, never took personal offence and never scored points. He told a crowd serenading him after his re-election in 1864, 'So long as I have been here I have not willingly planted a thorn in any man's bosom.'[6]

If Lincoln's persuasive control of his cabinet was integral to his pre-eminence as a policy (or non-policy) maker, so his relations with Congress were crucial to the prosecution of his policy. Without Congress, there would be no men and no money, and without them no war. Lincoln's insistence on the continuing democratic government meant that he had to carry both voters and the politicians with him at polls which were almost continuous – the House of Representatives is elected every two years, State governors and legislatures, city mayors and councils at regular but haphazardly spaced intervals. In a war in which every state was providing its sons for the army, every election reflected reactions to the ebb and flow of successes in the field. Lincoln's long experience of small-town life had left him with an uncanny sense of how opinion outside the hot-house of Congressional politics moved. He had to work through the politicians, but he knew that their concerns were often with their own ambitions and the hopes and fears of their party faithful (whom Lincoln had to keep loyal). What determined whether the war could be won would be the willingness of young men to fight and the enduring support which their families gave them.

From the beginning of his Presidency Lincoln established an 'open-door' policy at the White

House. Every day for two hours or more a motley
crowd passed through his office, haphazardly
screened by one of his two secretaries. Most came
to seek some Federal favour, military or civilian,
among the thousands of jobs created by the war and
all of which were, constitutionally, the President's
appointments, down to the lowliest postmaster.
There was no regular career structure for civil
service offices – all were political and each
appointment had to be made with a view to what its
political effect would be. Lincoln 'thought
sometimes that the only way he [could] escape from
them would be to take a rope and hang himself on
one of the trees in the lawn south of the president's
house'.[7] Relatives of serving men came seeking
their release on compassionate grounds and
petitioners sought pardon for deserters or military
delinquents about to be shot. He pardoned
hundreds of them against the inclination of
ministers and generals. He saw no purpose in
shooting a boy who had run home to see his mother
and he often expressed understanding of what he
called 'legs' cases, where it was not the soldier who
had deserted in battle, but his legs which had got
the better of him. Lincoln's manner was formal, but

he listened, his long legs crossed, an elbow on a knee, stroking his beard. For all he had gentle words and encouragement. Some came simply to shake his hand or wish him well; many brought him gifts, of fish, butter or, in one case, a maimed eagle. Many people thought Lincoln was wasting his time but he would not give up: he drew crucial knowledge from what he called his 'public opinion baths'.[8] His visitors usually carried away a warm regard which, bruited abroad, helped build up that popular support which cheered and cleansed him from the necessary machinations of the politician.

Lincoln's opponents accused him of aiming at a tyranny: he came to exert an almost dictatorial power but never swerved from observance of all the democratic and constitutional processes. His work day started in his office before breakfast and was followed, after his 'open door', by reading papers, signing documents and seeing ministers. After a light lunch (or none at all) he might ride, or drive with Mrs Lincoln, perhaps visiting soldiers' hospitals or a camp. After supper (he took no alcohol) he might return for another three hours in his office or walk alone without a guard, with a long grey shawl round his shoulders, to see what telegrams were coming in to the War Department, returning home around midnight, now too tired to engage in much conversation with Mary, which would have kept his marriage in a more congenial state. In summer the couple, business permitting, would spend nights at a Soldiers' Rest home outside Washington, where he could briefly rest, away from his worries.

SIX

THE OUTBREAK
OF CIVIL WAR

After the fall of Sumter the Union continued to disintegrate: Virginia (with the seat of Confederate government at Richmond, barely a hundred miles from Washington), North Carolina, Tennessee and Arkansas followed. The border slave states of Maryland and Delaware were held, and so, by swift military action, were Kentucky and Missouri. In the first years of the war, along with Virginia and Tennessee, they were the main theatres of war. Commanding the left bank of the Ohio and the right bank of the Mississippi, they were strategically crucial in maintaining access to Kansas and the West. Lincoln believed, 'to lose Kentucky is nearly the same as to lose the whole game.'[1] The worst fears of their inhabitants, expressed in their votes for either Douglas or the constitutional unionists in 1860, were to be borne out. Missouri and Kentucky remained deeply divided — 130,000 whites and 32,000 blacks from the two states fought in the Union armies, 65,000 for the Confederacy: Senator Crittenden of Kentucky had sons serving as generals in each army. Lincoln, who had grown up in just this world, bore the sorrows of the fratricidal slaughter as casualty lists brought in their news, and in his wife's divided sympathies.

The aims of the contesting governments differed. For the Confederacy it was a war of attrition to wear down Federal will to refuse it independence. For the Union the task was more paradoxical and difficult. The occasion of the war had been secession; the object of the war was to restore the Union; but the cause of the war was slavery. Yet, if rebellion was to be resisted successfully and the Union restored and the hated institution still survived, to what end the contest?

Lincoln acted swiftly after the fall of Sumter. He called for 75,000 volunteers (enthusiastically provided) to augment the tiny professional army of 14,000. He declared a total blockade of the whole of the rebel coastline, provided federal monies to help a New York committee for military measures and suspended *Habeas Corpus* in Federal areas where opposing armed forces were operating. After all these actions, which were constitutionally dubious in a situation in which Congress had not declared war, he called Congress into session – for 4 July 1861. Immediately the needs of the moment put great strains on continued constitutional rectitude. From the beginning Lincoln bravely acted on his military responsibility. If the Union and democracy were to be preserved by arms he must be the judge of the proper means to that end: 'Are all the laws, *but one* [*Habeas Corpus*], to go unexecuted, and the government itself go to pieces, lest that one be violated?'[2] More broadly he argued, 'I conceive that I may in an emergency do things on military grounds which cannot be done constitutionally by Congress.'[3]

When Congress met in July 1861, led by Crittenden from Kentucky, it confirmed the objects of war as Lincoln had defined them in his inaugural message: to defend and maintain the Union 'without overthrowing or interfering with the rights or established institutions of those States'. Lincoln made no demur: almost half of the votes cast in the free states in 1860 had not been cast for Lincoln. Northern Democrats had supported a party which had no objection to slavery. Any attempt to define the war aims to include freedom for slaves would destroy national unity just as the war was starting. Lincoln, unlike Jefferson Davis, the rebel president, was always to fight a war on two fronts. To win on the military front was a bloody emptiness if unity fell apart behind the lines; and the steely determination of a united people could mean nothing if the enemy was not defeated in the field. The two fronts were inextricably interwoven. Over-eager political pressure by radical Republicans for ending slavery and penalties for the rebels not only stirred up resistance from Peace Democrats and Conservatives, who were not averse to encouraging deserters, but also encouraged delay and procrastination by conservative generals in the field, many of them Democrats who preferred to fight a defensive war and aim for a negotiated restoration of unity. In a democratic state and with a volunteer army, every soldier had political views. Equally, success in battle, which excited the radical Republicans to push for more liberal war aims, drove conservatives further into hostility to the war and nearer to disloyalty. Opinion, expressed in a multitude of newspapers and in the regular elections, continually shifted and as Union armies gradually moved in to retake rebel territory the question of just how a reconstructed Union would look became the dominant question in politics. Waging peace and establishing its parameters ran in parallel with waging war. Every defeat for the army was blamed on the President's incompetence and lack of determination. Every victory created a new tangle of political problems in the incremental process of peace-making.

In Lincoln's eyes every rebel remained a Federal citizen and when the army occupied his farm he reassumed his rights as a citizen as soon as he took the oath of allegiance. In wars between sovereign states, the losers remain at the whim of their conquerors: they have no rights until they are determined by the final peace settlement. In this war peace went on parallel to the fighting. The loser, almost by the mere fact of losing, and seeking pardon, thought he was entitled to the same privileges under the Constitution as his vanquisher. Indeed, it seemed as though the loyal soldier was fighting to restore to his assailant just those rights and privileges his assailant had chosen to forego. Increasingly, soldiers resented having to restore to their owners fugitive slaves who had come into the Federal lines. At the same time, in the loyal border states and among conservatives, fear of any emancipation of the slaves only increased the wish for a negotiated peace and undermined the war effort. Lincoln, who saw himself as President for all Americans, Republican or Democrat, loyalist or rebel, had to weave his way through with endless patience, and avoiding all personal feeling, while at the same time overseeing operations in the field. A policy of no policy was not one calculated to arouse confident enthusiasm and the moment he showed decisiveness he was held to be partisan by his opponents, and reviled. The growth of the 'Lincoln Legend' after his death has obscured just how unpopular he was for much of his Presidency – not for his personal qualities but for his seeming incompetence at winning the war. At the end of 1861 Congress set up a Joint Committee on the Conduct of the War. Dominated by radical anti-slavery Republicans, it kept pressure on Lincoln to advance the cause of ending slavery. Increasingly, Congress suspected Lincoln was determining the shape of the future Union by making executive decisions without consulting it. The Constitution, assuming the Union to be perpetual, said nothing about reconstructing the Union; Lincoln, in his shaping of the future, relied on his military power and his pardoning power. Congress claimed responsibility for reconstruction, because it alone could admit elected representatives from redeemed states. As Lincoln said, 'If half the people think you have gone too far and the other half not far enough, you have probably done just about right'[4] – not a view which made for popularity or success at the polls.

All these problems which beset Lincoln every day were trivial compared with his responsibility for the conduct of the war, in which every casualty list, after a battle lost or won, brought the news of death to the homes of those whose support he must have for completing the task.

SEVEN

LINCOLN AND THE GENERALS

With few officers who had commanded more than a battalion, many of whom had trained with their Southern counterparts at West Point, without a general staff or command structure and with no experience himself, Lincoln at once had to command all the armed forces. For three years, a succession of disasters or inconclusive victories followed one another and casualties mounted. Lincoln sought an aggressive general who would seek the enemy out and destroy him. What he got were defensively minded professionals, good organizers but reluctant to fight unless forced. After a first disastrous encounter on 21 July 1861 at Bull Run, where the retreating Federal troops followed the scuttling picnickers who had come to see the fun back into nearby Washington, the front went quiet.

Lincoln's first commander in charge in Virginia after Bull Run, George McClellan, was overly cautious. The endless demand for reinforcements and his known Democrat views made him politically suspected and he had no objection to slavery. (Lincoln said sending reinforcements to McClellan was like shovelling fleas across a barnyard, so few of them seemed to get there.) But he was liked by his soldiers and Lincoln dared not remove him. In July 1862 Lincoln appointed Henry Halleck as General-in-Chief over McClellan. Halleck was supposed to advise Lincoln on military matters and act as the government's channel to the army, but 'Old Brains', as he was known, was only a good office soldier – he was unwilling to show initiative or take responsibility. Lincoln, knowing his own ignorance, contented himself with sending messages and encouragement rather than orders to his generals. In April 1862, when McClellan settled down to a siege of the Confederate capital, Richmond in Virginia, only 100 miles from Washington, Lincoln wrote to him: 'It is indispensable to *you* that you strike a blow. *I* am powerless to help this. . . . I have never written you . . . in greater kindness of feeling than now, nor with a fuller purpose to sustain you, so far as in my anxious *judgment*, I consistently can. *But you must act.*[1] After a second battle in Bull Run in August in which the army suffered 16,000 casualties, Lincoln in despair said at a cabinet meeting that 'he felt almost ready to hang himself'.[2] His visit to McClellan's army in July was recorded by a soldier:

> It did seem as though every moment the President's legs would become entangled with those of the horse he rode and both come down together. . . . The removal of his hat before each regiment was also a source of laughter . . . the quick trot of the horse making it a feat of some difficulty. . . . But the boys liked him. . . . His benign smile as he passed us by was a real reflection of his honest, kindly heart, but deeper, under the surface of that marked and not all uncomely face, were the signs of care and anxiety.[3]

At just this time Lincoln was pondering the problem of slavery. Already by May two Union generals had declared that slaves owned by rebel masters in their command should be free; Lincoln's repudiation of such insubordinate actions brought strong Northern condemnation at a time when the mid-term elections approached. The abolitionist leader, William Lloyd Garrison, declared that Lincoln 'has evidently not a drop of anti-slavery in his blood'. The initiative passed to Congress led by the Pennsylvania Radical, Thaddeus Steven: 'Free every slave – slay every trader – burn every Rebel mansion if these things are necessary to preserve the Temple of Liberty.'

In July 1862 Congress passed a Confiscation Act which provided for the confiscation of the property of all rebels; their slaves would be held as captives of war and forever free. Lincoln was now torn: he believed in the rigid observation of the Constitution, which denied to Congress any power over the internal institutions of the states (even in rebellion), and he believed that 'all men were created equal'. Ingeniously he saved his own neutrality by signing the bill but publishing his contemplated veto of it, thereby diverting conservative criticism on to Congress and avoiding a confrontation with the legislators.

Lincoln had begun having doubts in early 1862 as to whether slavery could survive the war. Since the constitution protected slavery its elimination could only be achieved by making abolition attractive. In

March he proposed to Congress that the loyal slave states should be offered gradual and compensated emancipation accompanied by a Federally funded and voluntary colonization of the freedmen and their families in a settlement in Central America. If the scheme worked Lincoln hoped that the example would convince the rebel states that slavery could be ended without material loss and without the danger of an ensuing race war. Congress unenthusiastically agreed. The border states did not: even those friendly to the proposals feared that if they were pressed it would lead to further secessions. Lincoln's initiative failed.

But Lincoln found another way forward: if Congress had no power over slavery, the President, acting from military necessity, did. After the failure of compensated emancipation and before the Confiscation Bill went through Congress, he had discussed with two Cabinet members a plan which would return the control over the future of slavery to himself and unlock the problem of liberated slaves by a Presidential proclamation. Later he discussed it with the cabinet, though he did not seek its assent. After McClellan at last produced a military victory at Antietam in the summer, Lincoln published his Emancipation Proclamation on 22 September 1862. The Proclamation was to come into effect after three months, on the first day of 1863: after this date all slaves in states still in rebellion would be free 'as a fit and necessary measure'. This left slavery still safe in the four slave states in the Union and said nothing about slavery in those former Confederate areas recaptured before the Proclamation came into force – not least New Orleans (taken in April 1862). Critics were quick to point out that the Proclamation only applied in areas where the government had no authority and that it did nothing about slavery where it had. Immediately, however, it solved the problem of its advancing troops who were increasingly loath to return liberated slaves to their masters, and it transformed a conservative war for 'the Union as it was' into a revolutionary struggle for freedom and a new nation vindicating its original basis for independence. Ambiguities were forgotten for the present (what happened when the war ended and the military justification for freeing the slaves lapsed? and what of the loyal slave states?). As Lincoln said in his December message to Congress,

> The dogmas of the quiet past are inadequate to the
> stormy present. . . . *We* cannot escape history. . . . The
> fiery trial through which we pass, will light us down,
> in honor or dishonor, to the latest generation. . . . In
> *giving* freedom to the *slave*, we *assure* freedom to the
> *free*. . . . We shall nobly save, or meanly lose, the last
> best, hope of earth.[4]

Lincoln knew that ending slavery would at once exacerbate the intractable problem of race relations, for which legislation could provide no solution. Though he hated slavery he had never believed that blacks were the same as whites, or that they could be happy living side by side. In his speech at Peoria in October 1854 he had admitted he saw no solution to the problem: 'My first impulse would be to free all the slaves, and send them to Liberia, – to their own native land . . . [but] its sudden execution is impossible. . . . What then? . . . Free them, and make them politically and socially, our equals? My own feelings . . . and . . . those of the great mass of white people will not [admit this].'[5] But the idea of separation remained with him.

In August 1862 he had an unprecedented meeting with a black delegation. In stark, plain terms he showed how conservative the views of a good liberal about blacks (as opposed to slavery) still were:

You and we are different races . . . [your race] suffer
very greatly, many of them by living among us, while
ours suffer from your presence. . . . Your race are
suffering . . . the greatest wrong inflicted on any
people. But even when you cease to be slaves, . . . not a
single man of your race is made the equal of a single
man of ours. . . . But for your race among us there
could not be war, although many men engaged on
either side do not care for you one way or the other. . . .
It is better for us both, therefore, to be separated.[6]

He exhorted them to give a lead to their people in
emigrating to their own country and starting a new
life. The delegation politely pointed out that they
already were in their own country. Lincoln's
attitude infuriated radicals who believed he should
rather have issued a 'manly protest against prejudice
against colour'. But they did not have the
responsibility of governing a country still
apprehensive about ending slavery: to have gone
further would have destroyed unity and comforted
their still powerful enemy.

Lincoln now slowly moved, cautiously as ever,
to recognizing that if blacks were to be free and
American they had to be integrated into society.
He had come under radical pressure after the

Proclamation to allow recruitment of freed slaves and free blacks into the army (a number of blacks already served in the navy), not least to ease the burden on white soldiers. Lincoln feared that they would not fight or would promote dissension in Union ranks, leading to massive desertion and perhaps to the secession of the border states. Nevertheless, in 1863 he started to encourage the enlistment of blacks, and the eagerness with which large numbers of them joined and fought went some little way to altering public presuppositions: 156,000 had enrolled by the end of the war. Later, unavailingly, he was to encourage rebel states to make some provision in their new constitutions for enfranchising better-educated blacks. Lincoln's views on slavery were fixed after 1854: his view of black men constantly evolved, partly from necessity and partly from his natural reflective appreciation of the part blacks were playing.

After January 1863 the nature of the war changed: as Lincoln said to a visitor, 'From the expiration of the days of grace [to 1 January] the character of the war will be changed. It will be one of extermination and subjugation.' McClellan, who was opposed to the Emancipation Proclamation, had finally been removed in November 1862. New generals had no greater success in the field in the East and the strain on Lincoln told. He was refreshed by a visit to the Army of the Potomac in April but, as he said, 'nothing could touch the tired spot within, which was all tired'.[7] After another disaster, with 17,000 Union casualties, at Chancellorsville in May, the greatest victory of the Confederate commander, Robert E. Lee, Lincoln was appalled: 'What will the country say? Oh, what will the country say?'[8]

In the West, however, the tide was turning. For a year Grant had been attempting to free the Mississippi and so cut the Confederacy off from its Western states, Louisiana, Arkansas and Texas. Admiral Farragut took New Orleans from the sea in April 1862. A year later, after a long siege and brilliant campaign, the Northern general, Ulysses S. Grant, took Vicksburg in July 1863. Lincoln rejoiced: 'The Father of Waters again goes unvexed to the sea.'[9] He had found his general. He had been hesitant at Grant's bold plan for taking Vicksburg, but now he declared, 'Grant is mine and I am his for the rest of the war.'

In the East, Lee, to ease pressure on the West, struck north into Pennyslvania, carrying the war into the enemy's territory. On 1 July 1863, after more Federal changes of generals, the two armies met at Gettysburg. After two days of savage fighting, the Confederate army yielded the field. It turned out to have been the decisive battle of the war, but Lincoln was distraught that Lee had been allowed to get away. He wrote to the successful General Meade, '[The enemy] was within your easy grasp, and to have closed upon him would, in connection with our other successes, have ended the war.'[10] But he never sent this letter to Meade. Again and again Lincoln's letters to his generals spelt out the strategy which, at last, Grant was to adopt: that the destruction of the enemy's forces was all, not the capture of cities or a defensive victory in battle. 'If our army can not fall upon the enemy and hurt him where he is,' he wrote, '. . . it can gain nothing by attempting to follow him over a succession of intrenched lines into a fortified city.'[11] In September, Lincoln appointed Grant as commanding officer of all operations between the Appalachians and the Mississippi. His continuing victories paid a handsome political dividend to the

Republican party in the state election in the autumn: conscription had been introduced in March, provoking the worst riots in America's history (120 blacks died in New York city) and encouraging anti-war Democratic judges and justices (known as Copperheads) to obstruct the process and foster desertions. Lincoln replied strongly to his critics, who said that he was now fighting a war simply in the interests of the blacks. In a private letter, made public, he wrote, 'You say you will not fight to free negroes. Some of them seem willing to fight for you. . . . If they stake their lives for us, they must be prompted by the strongest motive – even the promise of freedom. . . . [When peace comes it] will then have been proved that, among free men, there can be no successful appeal from the ballot to the bullet.'[12] The Republicans had resounding successes in the elections.

Lincoln was an assiduous correspondent; all letters, on whatever subject, were answered, most often in longhand. In his years in office he had no holiday and little time for personal correspondence: his private life, such as it was, he found in his family. His tenderness is glimpsed in letters and telegrams to Mary when she was out of town. In these uneasy months of August he wrote to her, 'Tell dear Tad, poor "Nanny Goat", is lost. . . . The day you left Nanny was found resting herself, and chewing her little cud, on the middle of Tad's bed. But now she's gone! . . . This is the last we know of poor "Nanny".'[13] The same tenderness of tone and the sense of what the war was costing thousands of families and why it was a price worth paying comes through in the most famous of his speeches, at once grand and universal and intimate.

EIGHT

THE END OF THE REBELLION

In November Lincoln was invited to say a few words at the dedication of a war cemetery on the battlefield of Gettysburg in Pennsylvania. He accepted and took great trouble with what he should say; he was still working on its conclusion when he left Washington by special train. Mrs Lincoln wished him not to go because Tad was ill that morning but Lincoln insisted that he must. For two hours he sat on the platform listening to the main orator, a former president of Harvard who spoke without notes. Lincoln then stood up, put on his glasses and, holding a single sheet of notes, spoke for less than two minutes. When he sat down a press photographer was still fumbling with his equipment. Lincoln thought his speech had failed — turning to a friend he said, 'that speech won't scour' (turning over the heavy prairie soil with a good plough).[1] In fact he had delivered the most famous speech in American history. In fewer than three hundred words he caught the pathos of war and the hope for the future of liberty in it. Simple words spell out how Americans understood their place and responsibilities in the great scheme of things. It remains unsurpassed in its beauty and its truths.

Four score and seven years ago our fathers brought forth on this continent, a new nation, conceived in Liberty, and dedicated to the proposition that all men are created equal.

Now we are engaged in a great civil war, testing whether that nation, or any nation so conceived and so dedicated, can long endure. We are met on a great battle-field of that war. We have come to dedicate a portion of that field, as a final resting place for those who here gave their lives that that nation might live. It is altogether fitting and proper that we should do this.

But, in a larger sense, we can not dedicate — we can not consecrate — we can not hallow — this ground. The brave men, living and dead, who struggled here, have consecrated it, far above our poor power to add or detract. The world will little note, nor long remember what we say here, but it can never forget what they did here. It is for us the living, rather, to be dedicated here to the unfinished work which they who fought here have thus far so nobly advanced. It is rather for us to be here dedicated to the great task remaining before us – that from these honored dead we take increased devotion to that cause for which they gave the last full measure of devotion – that we here highly resolve that these dead shall not have died in vain – that this nation, under God, shall have a new birth of freedom – and that government of the people, by the people, for the people, shall not perish from the earth.[2]

The birth of the new nation was 1776 (the Declaration of Independence) not 1787 (the Constitution which protected slavery). There is no reference to the rebels or to slavery. He talked of the nation (five times), not of the state, which alone could bring to fulfilment the Federal conception. And he looked beyond America 'to any other nation so conceived'. If America failed, all might fail and freedom perish from the earth. The architecture of the whole text matched the nobility of the sentiment: short words, simple sentences, single adjectives. The repeated opening words of successive sentences ring out like the tolling of the passing bell, both remembering the fallen and calling the living to vindicate their death. He said nothing of the future when the fighting stopped. But as military successes gave hope of ultimate victory, Lincoln could no longer avoid making provision for reconstruction.

From his return from the Gettysburg ceremony until his re-election a year later, Lincoln fought to retain the initiative on the shape of reconstruction. The bitter conflict with Congress over Lincoln's determination on a lenient and reconciliatory remaking of the Union brought the President to the verge of defeat, from which he was, in great measure, saved by Grant's success in the war – so closely did politics and warfare influence each other.

Lincoln's Proclamation of Amnesty and Reconstruction for Louisiana and Tennessee,[3] issued on 8 December 1863, relied on the presidential pardoning power: when 10 per cent of those who had voted in the last Federal election in 1860 had taken the oath of allegiance (and accepted Lincoln's proclamation about slavery), they could draw up a new prospective constitution and apply to Congress for readmission. Their property, less slaves, would be restored. Many radicals in the Republican party resisted such lenient terms, the most radical wanting the distribution of confiscated lands as land-grants for the freed slaves to ensure their economic independence. A bill passed by Congress in July 1864 required 50 per cent of the 1860 voters to take a retrospective oath, that they had never willingly taken up arms against the Federal government. The effect of such severe requirements would almost certainly postpone readmission until after the end of hostilities – when Lincoln's extraordinary war powers would automatically lapse. Ingeniously, Lincoln did not veto the bill (which with a two-thirds majority Congress could override); he simply failed to sign it before Congress rose (so that the bill automatically failed). Lincoln thus marginalized the role of Congress in reconstruction (though, as their refusal of Louisiana's application for admission under Lincoln's Proclamation showed, they retained a power to veto). Lincoln would never contemplate the radicals' proposals for a massive redistribution of property. The ending of slavery without compensation was already the most revolutionary attack on private property in European history: to go further would have been to anticipate the Russian October Revolution of 1917.

Lincoln's quarrel with Congress coincided with the campaign for his re-election and the return of defeats in the field. Lincoln himself was convinced by late summer 1864 that he would not be re-elected and in the end his success owed much to Grant's successes in the field. In March Lincoln had appointed Grant as General-in-Chief of all the armies. Grant performed everything Lincoln had been seeking for three years: he saw that the destruction of the rebel armies was the objective, he attacked them on several fronts at once and he never let up. Though he fought a series of bloody battles with huge casualties in the summer in Virginia (little more successful than his pre-decessors) he refused to go on the defensive. After the battles of the Wilderness in May 1864, when the army suffered 32,000 casualties in two weeks, Grant had told Stanton, the Secretary for War, 'I propose to fight it out on this line if it takes all summer.'⁴ Lincoln was all but overcome with grief. The Speaker of the House found him 'his long arms behind his back, his dark features contracted still more with gloom as he exclaimed "Why do we suffer reverses after reverses? Could we have avoided this terrible, bloody war? Was it not forced upon us? Is it ever to end?"'[5] But he never lost faith in Grant who was now under heavy criticism on account of his losses in men.

Mid-summer was a time of great crisis. Lincoln believed that, though he had been renominated in June, he might still be ousted by the party. Worse, he feared that, if he lost, whoever replaced him would negotiate a peace in which either the independence of the Confederacy would be acknowledged or slavery retained. The attempt to replace him as Republican candidate hurt him deeply – 'to be wounded in the house of one's friends is perhaps the most grievous affliction that can befall a man'[6] – but he would make no concessions. He would not go back on the Emancipation Proclamation and he would not bow to radical demands for stiffer penalties for the rebels. He maintained an ambiguity which suggests that he himself was uncertain of the best way forward. He aborted negotiations proposed by Confederate agents in Canada by insisting on the abandonment of slavery as a condition for talks. A month later, in August, he wrote to a Democrat, who deplored the insistence on an end to slavery, on the military impossibility of going back on the Emancipation Proclamation, ending the letter, 'If

Jefferson Davis wishes . . . to know what I would do if he were to offer peace and re-union, saying nothing about slavery, let him try me.'[7] Again Lincoln never signed nor sent the letter. He discussed such a possibility with the chairman of the National Republican Committee, but they agreed that to enter talks with slavery an open question would be to accept defeat.

By late August the tide began to turn. The Democrats took General McClellan, Lincoln's old commander, as their candidate but he repudiated their platform which called for immediate efforts for an armistice, to be followed by a convention to produce a peace 'on the basis of the Federal Union of the States' – nothing was said about slavery. By astute politicking Lincoln defused the movement to run a candidate against him from inside the Republican party and at last Grant fulfilled his promise. On 2 September Grant wired Lincoln, 'Atlanta is ours, and fairly won'[8] – the central dispersal point of the Confederate war machine had fallen. Lincoln took every political advantage of the military situation: generals were encouraged to give soldiers leave to vote in state elections. In New York radical Federal customs officials were replaced by conservatives to bring that most conservative of states into line.

On polling day Lincoln carried all but three states – New Jersey, Kentucky and Delaware – and increased his share of the popular vote to 55 per cent. The Republicans increased their hold on Congress. Lincoln had kept all his options open and was now free to go forward. Grant's victory in Atlanta had probably been the decisive moment. In 1860 the voter had answered a political question: the continuance of the Union. In 1864 the issue was a moral one about the nature of that Union. Lincoln's skill in holding the machinations of the politicians in check and relying on the ordinary voter to complete the unfinished work of the Gettysburg address was a measure of his statesmanship and intuition. Of the soldiers, those who bore the heat of the day, 78 per per cent had voted for Lincoln. James Russell Lowell reflected on 'a long-headed and long-purposed man [who had] shown from the first the considerate wisdom of a practical statesman'.[9]

But the 44 per cent who voted for McClellan showed a society still as divided about the future as it had been in 1860. When the old Congress (elected in 1862) met, it passed the Thirteenth Amendment, abolishing slavery, which Lincoln sent to the states for ratification (by a three-quarters majority) on 31 January 1865. By April only the states which voted for McClellan had failed to ratify; the rebel states were all required to ratify as a condition of readmission. At last, the deep flaw in the original Constitution was removed.

Military successes continued. On 22 December 1864 Grant telegraphed to the President, 'I beg to present you as a Christmas gift the city of Savannah'[10] after Sherman's blind march with an army of 62,000, unheard of for thirty-two days, from 'Atlanta to the sea'. At the same time the rebel army, attempting to reach Lee in Virginia from the West, was destroyed at Nashville in Tennessee. Lee was finally brought to bay on 9 April 1865 when, at Appomattox Court House, in full dress uniform, he surrendered to Grant who was wearing his old battle dress with its trousers tucked into his muddy boots. Three days before Lincoln had visited Richmond and pondered as he sat at Jefferson Davis's desk. A black man cried out in triumph, 'I know I am free for I have seen Father Abraham and felt him.'

In his second Inaugural Message, with the end in sight, Lincoln showed how deeply he saw the whole tragedy of the war: no note of triumph, no word of recrimination, only a recognition of the just and inscrutable ways of a God he had increasingly come to sense working in history and to whom it was men's task to bow.

Let us judge not that we be not judged. . . . Fondly do we hope – fervently do we pray – that this mighty scourge of war may speedily pass away. Yet, if God wills that it continue, until all the wealth piled by the bond-man's two hundred and fifty years of unrequited toil shall be sunk, and until every drop of blood drawn with the lash, shall be paid by another drawn with the sword . . . so still it must be said 'the judgments of the Lord, are true and righteous altogether'. With malice towards none, with charity for all . . . let us strive on to finish the work we are in; to bind up the nation's wounds; . . . to do all which may achieve and cherish a just, and a lasting, peace, among ourselves, and with all nations.[11]

After a cabinet meeting in the morning of 14 April and a drive with Mary in the afternoon, Lincoln was in excellent spirits. In the evening he went to the theatre, one of the few relaxations he had enjoyed during the war. In the third act a single shot rang out and an unsuccessful actor, John Wilkes Booth, leapt from the President's box to the stage and escaped through the dressing-rooms. Lincoln lingered through the night and died the following morning, surrounded by his wife and most of his cabinet. After prayers were said, Stanton, raising an arm as though in farewell, said, 'Now he belongs to the ages.'

NINE

LINCOLN IN HISTORY

The annals of the past contain few accounts of truly good men. Historians are more used to analysing a mixture of ingredients, good and bad intentions, success and failure, high endeavours threatened by flaws in execution, and to balance out the sums ending with a careful plus or minus. Lincoln is rare in providing much for history to ponder and reflect on but little to dispute with except in the shortcomings in the execution of his policies. He is the rarer for his absolute success through four years of bitter politics and bloody warfare. He sought power, without pretending otherwise, and exercised it to the full; he gave credit for success to others and accepted the responsibility for his own failures. But he is singular, perhaps unique in history, in that he was never corrupted by power. His ambition was tied not to personal gain but to a pair of succeeding

and complementary principles: to restore a nation
dedicated to the proposition that 'all men are
created equal' and to ensure that a union so
recovered was purged of the great contradiction
which had lain at the heart of its constitution. His
loyalty to government by consent required that he
could only achieve his aims if his fellow citizens
agreed with him and could be held to their purpose
through the darkest hours. In that art of persuasion
he was a consummate politician, subtly and
ruthlessly working the levers of parties and
politicians to achieve a balance between the
fractions and factions of competing groups and
ideas, whose particular interests threatened to
destroy the precarious patriotism which sustained
the army. He listened, avoided argument, kept his
counsel, and then he made his decisions from which
he would not diverge. His skill in reconciling
oppositions and commanding their respect grew
from his apprenticeship in the little rural
communities where he had learned to make his way
through the full diversity of the world, and from his
long reflective self-observation in times of
depression, which gave him the same sympathetic
insight into the character of others that he had into

himself. As the war continued and the casualty figures grew, he found a convinced agnostic faith that there was some divine purpose in the affairs of men, though he could not define or confine the deity within any Christian confession. A man must observe the ebb and flow of events and act on what he can discern in the tides. He had no faith that man could deflect God from his course.

Lincoln's humility about his own capabilities saved him from jealous rivalries or disputes: he saw sincerity even in the views of his bitterest critics and in the rebel leaders. He infuriated his supporters and enemies alike by his apparent dithering when decisive action was needed, but he turned their strictures into constructive advice from which, in the end, he evolved his decisions. He had had to teach himself the job of being president in the most challenging moment in the nation's history and as he learned so he commanded more and more personal respect. He died with the noblest part of the great task achieved – the end of slavery. The very near religious veneration in which he was held at his death grew rapidly in the dark days of reconstruction when the new government attempted to complete the job by defining a meaning for freedom and equality which now included all Americans. The legend as it grew obscured the real man but the core of the story is true and the achievements of the greatest President remain unchallenged and untarnished. He ensured the survival of 'the last best hope of earth' – popular government and the rule of law. Without Lincoln's presidency the fortunes of all other nations 'so conceived in liberty' would have been at risk and the rest of the free world would have been left on its own to face the dark forces which ravaged the globe in the twentieth century.

Notes and References

Chapter One

1. Roy P. Basler (ed.), *The Collected Works of Abraham Lincoln*, 1953–55 (hereafter *CW*) IV: 271.
2. *CW* I: 378.
3. *CW* VI: 16–17.
4. Quoted in David Donald, *Lincoln*, 1995, p. 271.

Chapter Two

1. *CW* III: 512.
2. *CW* I: 75.
3. *CW* I: 261.

Chapter Three

1. *CW* I: 307.
2. *CW* II: 4.
3. *CW* II: 129.
4. *CW* III: 512.
5. *CW* II: 245.
6. *CW* II: 255.
7. *CW* II: 266.

Chapter Four

1. *CW* II: 461.
2. *CW* III: 322.
3. *CW* III: 177–8.
4. *CW* III: 274–5.

5. *CW* III: 311.
6. *CW* III: 16.
7. *CW* III: 279.
8. *CW* III: 395.
9. *CW* IV: 45.
10. *CW* IV: 34.
11. Richard N. Current, *The Lincoln Nobody Knows*, 1958, p. 202.
12. *CW* IV: 129.

CHAPTER FIVE

1. *CW* IV: 183 and 150.
2. *CW* IV: 268.
3. H.S. Commager (ed.), *Documents of American History*, vol. I, 7th edn 1963, p. 392.
4. *CW* IV: 317.
5. Quoted in D.E. and V. Fehrenbacher (eds), *Recollected Words of Abraham Lincoln*, 1996, p. 351.
6. *CW* VIII: 101.
7. Fehrenbacher, *Recollected Words*, p. 504.
8. Quoted in Donald, *Lincoln*, p. 391.

CHAPTER SIX

1. *CW* IV: 532.
2. *CW* IV: 430.
3. Fehrenbacher, *Recollected Words*, p. 228.
4. Quoted in J.M. McPherson, *Ordeal by Fire*, vol. II, *The Civil War*, 1982, p. 262.

CHAPTER SEVEN

1. *CW* V: 185.
2. Fehrenbacher, *Recollected Words*, p. 28.
3. Quoted in B. Thomas, *Abraham Lincoln*, 1963, p. 214–15.
4. *CW* V: 537.
5. *CW* II: 255–6.
6. *CW* V: 371–2.
7. Fehrenbacher, *Recollected Words*, p. 42.

8.   Fehrenbacher, *Recollected Words*, p. 44.
9.   *CW* VI: 409.
10. *CW* VI: 328.
11. *CW* VI: 467.
12. *CW* VI: 409–10.
13. *CW* VI: 371–2.

CHAPTER EIGHT

1.   Fehrenbacher, *Recollected Words*, p. 289.
2.   *CW* VII: 23.
3.   Commager, *Documents*, pp. 429–31.
4.   Donald, *Lincoln*, p. 501.
5.   Fehrenbacher, *Recollected Words*, p. 113.
6.   Fehrenbacher, *Recollected Words*, p. 48.
7.   *CW* VII: 501.
8.   Donald, *Lincoln*, p. 530.
9.   Donald, *Lincoln*, p. 543.
10. Thomas, *Abraham Lincoln*, p. 320.
11. *CW* VIII: 333.

SELECT
BIBLIOGRAPHY

For a brilliant and most readable survey of the whole period
of crisis, 1845–65, see McPherson, James, *Ordeal by Fire*,
3 vols, (vol. I *The Coming of the War*, vol. II *The Civil War*, vol. III
Reconstruction), New York, Knopf, 1982.

The best of the innumerable lives of Lincoln are Donald,
David H., *Lincoln*, London, Cape, 1995 and Thomas,
Benjamin P., *Abraham Lincoln: A biography*, London, Eyre and
Spottiswoode, 1953.

Current, Richard N., *The Lincoln Nobody Knows*, New York,
Toronto, London, McGraw-Hill, 1958, offers shrewd
assessments of Lincoln's qualities as President and
Commander-in-Chief.

Basler, Roy P. (ed.), *The Collected Works of Abraham Lincoln*,
9 vols, New Brunswick, New Jersey, Rutgers University
Press, 1953–55, are indispensable for the serious scholar.
Two additional volumes, 10 and 11, round up remaining
odds and ends (1990–4). Harriet Beecher Stowe's *Uncle Tom's
Cabin*, 1853, though neither literature nor sound sociology,
does not entirely belie Lincoln's supposed remark to its
author: 'Is this the little woman who made the great war?'
No comparable literary justification of slavery appeared from
the South.

Select Bibliography

See also:

Commager, H.S. (ed.), *Documents of American History*, vol. I. New York, Appleton-Century-Crofts, 7th edn, 1963.

Fehrenbacher, D.E. and V. (ed), *Recollected Words of Abraham Lincoln*, Stanford, California, Stanford University Press, 1996.

POCKET BIOGRAPHIES

AVAILABLE

Beethoven
Anne Pimlott Baker

Scott of the Antarctic
Michael De-la-Noy

Alexander the Great
E.E. Rice

Sigmund Freud
Stephen Wilson

Marilyn Monroe
Sheridan Morley and
Ruth Leon

Rasputin
Harold Shukman

Jane Austen
Helen Lefroy

Mao Zedong
Delia Davin

Ellen Terry
Moira Shearer

Abraham Lincoln
H.G. Pitt

David Livingstone
C.S. Nicholls

Charles Dickens
Catherine Peters

FORTHCOMING

Marie and Pierre Curie
John Senior

Margot Fonteyn
Alastair Macaulay

Winston Churchill
Robert Blake

Enid Blyton
George Greenfield

FORTHCOMING

George IV
Michael De-la-Noy

Christopher Wren
James Chambers

W.G. Grace
Donald Trelford

Che Guevara
Andrew Sinclair

Joseph Stalin
Harold Shukman

J.B. Priestley
Michael Denison

Lawrence of Arabia
Jeremy Wilson

Christopher Columbus
Peter Rivière

For a copy of our complete list or details of other Sutton titles, please contact Regina Schinner at Sutton Publishing Limited, Phoenix Mill, Thrupp, Stroud, Gloucestershire, GL5 2BU